NUCLEAR ENERGY

NUCLEAR ENERGY

BY DAN HALACY
Revised by
NORMAN SCHREIBER

A GROLIER COMPANY

A First Book ■ Revised Edition
FRANKLIN WATTS ■ 1984
New York ■ London ■ Toronto ■ Sydney

Diagrams by Vantage Art, Inc.

Photographs courtesy of: Department of Energy: opposite p. 1, p. 30; Defense Nuclear Agency: p. 4; Harlingue, The Niels Bohr Library: p. 7; Los Alamos Scientific Laboratory for Department of Energy: p. 8; Brookhaven National Laboratory: p. 11; Tennessee Valley Authority: p. 13; UPI: pp. 16, 40, 50, 57, 64; AP/Wide World: pp. 17, 46; Atomic Industrial Forum: p. 20, 21; Commonwealth Edison: p. 31; Superphénix-French Embassy: p. 37; Electric Power Research Institute: p. 54; GA Technologies Inc.: p. 60; Pam Am-Defense Nuclear Agency: p. 68; Sandia Laboratories: p. 73 (top and bottom).

Library of Congress Cataloging in Publication Data

Halacy, D. S. (Daniel Stephen), 1919–
Nuclear energy.

(A First book)
Bibliography: p.
Includes index.
Summary: Discusses nuclear energy, its production, use, and risks involved in its utilization.
1. Atomic power—Juvenile literature.
2. Atomic power plants—Juvenile literature.
[1. Atomic power. 2. Atomic power plants]
I. Schreiber, Norman. II. Title.
TK9148.H34 1984   621.48'3   84-7361
ISBN 0-531-04829-2

CONTENTS

NUCLEAR
ENERGY

THE POWER
INSIDE
THE ATOM

All matter is a collection of very tiny separate particles known as **atoms**. At one time, scientists thought that the atom was the smallest unit of matter. In fact, our word "atom" comes from the Greek word *atomos*, meaning "indivisible." Today, we know there are even smaller particles. However, atoms are the smallest units of matter showing all the characteristics that make up a particular chemical **element**, and these are what make up our world. There are 106 known elements, including many you probably have heard of—gold, silver, oxygen, carbon, uranium, and so on. Large numbers of similar atoms join together to form each of the various elements.

You also may have heard the term **molecules**. Molecules are larger subunits of matter. A molecule may be composed of a group of identical atoms linked together to form an element, or it may consist of two or more different kinds of atoms linked together to form a chemical compound. For example, in the chemical compound we call water, every single molecule is made up of two hydrogen atoms and one oxygen atom. Written symbols are used to represent the elements; the symbol for a molecule of water is H_2O.

Atoms are so small that even under very powerful microscopes only the largest ones can be seen. Yet the atom itself is merely a "container." Inside is the structure called the **nucleus**. Within this nucleus is the real world of nuclear energy. An atom's nucleus is composed of smaller particles known as **protons** and **neutrons**. These are packed very tightly together. In fact, that energy which holds them together is the source of nuclear energy. Particles called **electrons** travel around the nucleus. For a long time, scientists thought electrons moved around an atom's nucleus as the planets in our solar system move around the sun. Recent research indicates this may not be so.

Around the turn of the twentieth century it was discovered that protons and electrons are electrically charged. Protons carry a positive charge and electrons a negative charge. Neutrons weren't discovered until later, and eventually they were found to have no charge at all.

The atoms of all elements are made from the same materials, but in different proportions. What makes the atoms of one element different from those of any other element is the number of subatomic particles they contain. Each element's atoms contain a unique number of protons and electrons. For example, the nucleus of every single atom in a piece of gold contains seventy-nine protons. Every carbon atom has six. The number of protons and electrons in the atoms of a given element never changes. And there is always the same number of protons as electrons. Gold, for example, has seventy-nine protons and seventy-nine electrons. This number, 79, is referred to as gold's atomic number. Carbon's atomic number is 6.

For neutrons, however, the situation is quite different. The number of neutrons in a particular element is usually constant—but not always. When the number of neutrons in an element's nucleus is not the number usually found there, we have an **isotope**, a different form of the element.

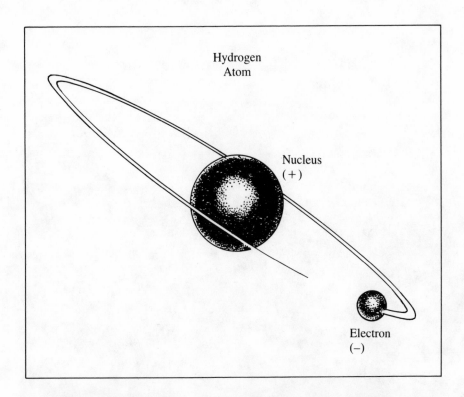

Hydrogen
Atom

Nucleus
(+)

Electron
(−)

To get a sense of what an atom may look like, think of a diagram of the solar system. Our solar system takes up a huge volume in space. Most of this volume is empty of solid matter. It is the same inside the atom. It also might help to think of an atom tremendously enlarged to the size of the Houston Astrodome. Picture a marble resting on the 50-yard line. The marble represents the atom's nucleus. It is from the tiny nucleus that nuclear power plants provide us with the energy for creating electricity.

THE NUCLEAR AGE

Nuclear energy is our newest source of power for mass consumption. (There have been promising results from experiments in new

techniques in solar and wind energy, but so far none has yet been able to yield much power for many people.) Nuclear energy does not yet produce nearly as much energy as coal, natural gas, or petroleum. Still, the chances are about one in eight that your lights, television set, and other appliances get their electricity from one of the nearly eighty nuclear power plants in the United States.

Nuclear power is one result of the Nuclear Age, which began only about forty years ago. It began with the development and use of a highly destructive weapon, the atomic bomb. First exploded near the end of World War II, atomic bombs demonstrated an awesome power. The two dropped on Japan caused that country to surrender almost immediately. Scientists who helped develop these superweapons felt that atomic power also might be used for peaceful purposes. This view was part of a tradition of applying the latest technology to human needs.

Two hundred years ago, humankind learned that wood, coal, oil, and natural gas—all of which produce energy when burned—could be used to run machines. Thus began what was called the Machine Age or the Industrial Revolution. Nuclear energy, a completely different kind of energy, is not produced by the burning of fuel. How then is it produced?

DISCOVERY OF
RADIOACTIVITY AND
NUCLEAR ENERGY

Nuclear energy was discovered by accident. In 1896, a French scientist, Antoine Henri Becquerel, was experimenting with uranium salts. These salts were known to "fluoresce," or give off a light

The nuclear age began with a weapon.
This picture shows Hiroshima
after the explosion of the atomic bomb.

of their own when exposed to sunlight. One day Becquerel put some uranium salt crystals on a photographic film. He wanted to study the uranium in the sunlight. It was cloudy outside, so he put the film away.

He returned to the film a few days later. At that time, he found the uranium actually had given off a stream of rays from inside itself without sunlight or any other outside help. These rays were called "Becquerel rays" in honor of their discoverer. Becquerel's rays fascinated two other scientists in France, Marie and Pierre Curie. In 1898, Marie Curie named the phenomenon **radioactivity**. The Curies' experiments led to the discovery of two new elements—**radium** and polonium—each with even greater radioactive power. In 1903, the Curies and Becquerel shared the Nobel Prize for discovering radioactivity. Marie Curie is still remembered today in the word **curie**, the term used to measure the amount of radiation emitted by 1 gram (.04 oz) of radium.

For hundreds of years, people believed the atom was a solid particle that could not be further broken down. They viewed it as the basic "building block" of nature. However, as a result of the work done by Becquerel and the Curies, scientists learned that some atoms break down naturally, though very slowly. As an atom breaks down, it issues a stream of radioactive rays, or energy, from inside the nucleus. These rays are the **binding energy** holding the nucleus together.

In 1904, the British scientist Ernest Rutherford wrote that if we could cause the disintegration of an atom, the result would be a release of an enormous amount of energy. This energy might then be tapped for our use. But by 1937, the year of his death, Rutherford doubted that any practical use ever would be made of the

Marie and Pierre Curie in
their laboratory in 1896.

The kind of bomb that hit Hiroshima. It was 28 inches across and 120 inches long. It had the effect of 20,000 tons of high explosives.

energy within the atom. However, new research, already under way, would soon lead to the Nuclear Age's real beginning.

THE ATOM BOMB

In 1939 an experiment was reported in which some European scientists "bombarded" a tiny bit of uranium with a stream of neutrons. The neutrons penetrated the nucleus and caused the uranium atom to split into two new atoms. The process was called **fission**. These new atoms were found to be atoms of the elements barium and krypton—not atoms of uranium!

These scientists succeeded in doing what others had only dreamed about. They changed one element into other elements. Uranium does change to other elements naturally, but the natural process takes many millions of years. Artificial fission on the other hand happens almost instantaneously.

Transforming one element into another by fission was a long-sought-after miracle. Something else was even more miraculous. In splitting, the uranium atom released the energy within its nucleus exactly as Rutherford had predicted. Moreover the amount of energy was tremendous. Nuclear fission released *seven million times* the energy produced in the burning of a carbon atom! Science had accidentally unlocked the key to an energy storehouse far beyond the imagination of the time.

While this was going on, Adolf Hitler and the Nazi regime had taken control of Germany. Hitler set out to dominate the world by means of ruthless military conquest. Fearing that Nazi Germany was about to enslave Europe, Italy's Enrico Fermi, as well as other scientists from many countries, came to America to work on what they called an **atomic pile**. Now it's usually called a **nuclear reactor** or just a **reactor.** They carefully assembled several tons of uranium in a squash court in a University of Chicago sports stadium. In 1942, they created a fission reaction that was "self-sustaining."

Sufficient uranium fuel was placed in the atomic pile to create what is called a critical mass. At this point, neutrons escaping naturally from the uranium atoms struck other atoms in the fuel. Each bombarding neutron produced another neutron from within the nucleus of a uranium atom. This process continued in a **chain reaction,** and the massive release of neutrons freed tremendous amounts of energy.

In 1945, at a secret military base in New Mexico, the first atom bomb was exploded. It used just a few kilograms (1 kg = 2.2 lb) of a uranium isotope known as uranium 235. That small amount had a power equal to tens of thousands of kilograms of the most powerful explosives.

Soon after the testing, two similar bombs met their targets, the Japanese cities of Hiroshima and Nagasaki. One bomb nearly destroyed the entire city of Hiroshima and killed or wounded some 130,000 people. The other bomb destroyed one-third of Nagasaki and left 75,000 dead or wounded.

Uranium could be a source of great destruction. But, it also had constructive possibilities: just a single kilogram of uranium has the energy of about 3,000 tons of coal, which is used in producing electricity. The next question was, why not use nuclear energy instead of coal?

ATOMS FOR PEACE

Even during wartime, scientists and engineers were planning to use nuclear power for peaceful purposes. Soon after the war, the United States formed its Atomic Energy Commission to manage the nuclear energy effort. (The AEC was disbanded in 1974. Its functions were divided between the Nuclear Regulatory Commission and the Department of Energy.) Scientists and technicians developed uses for nuclear materials in agriculture, industry, and most important, medicine. Today, many people owe their health and even their lives to treatment with nuclear medicine.

President Dwight D. Eisenhower made "Atoms for Peace" a national goal in 1954. The Nuclear Age, which began with destruc-

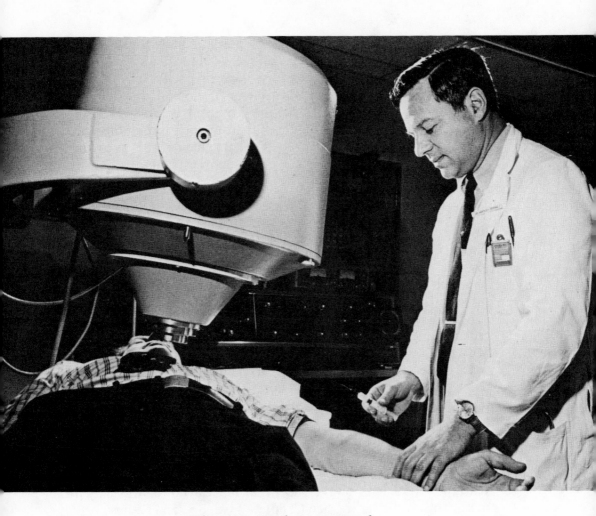

*The patient is being injected
with a radioacive isotope
substance. By tracing the
movement of the isotope,
the doctor will be able
to detect heart disease.*

tion, soon applied the tiny atom's great power to more constructive uses. In the Bible, the prophet Isaiah speaks of turning swords into plowshares. Thus the first peacetime use of nuclear power was dubbed Project Plowshare. It consisted of developing explosives to blast excavation sites for construction projects. Nuclear explosions were used later to obtain natural gas from rock formations too dense for normal drilling. The most exciting idea of all was to use nuclear energy itself to drive our electric power plants.

NUCLEAR ELECTRICITY

In 1951, an experimental nuclear power plant began operating in Idaho. Within three years it was providing all the electricity for the town of Arco. In 1957, a small commercial nuclear power plant was built at Shippingport, Pennsylvania. This plant produced 90 megawatts of electric power for Pittsburgh. (A megawatt is 1,000,000 watts.) Ninety megawatts is not very much electric power. Later, plants were built with larger capability. The nuclear plant at Brown's Ferry, Alabama, for example, produces 3,000 megawatts of electricity, more than the largest fossil-fuel electric power plant in America. This equals thirty-three times the megawatts produced at the Shippingport plant, and provides electricity for a million people.

Today, we get about 12 percent of our electricity from nuclear energy. Some energy experts have predicted that as much as 40 percent of our electric power may come from nuclear energy by the year 2000. (Others, however, feel that nuclear power will play a minor role in the future. See Chapters Five, Six, and Seven.)

The first reactor, delivered to Browns Ferry, Alabama. The plant produces more electricity than the largest fossil fuel plant in the United States.

JOBS IN NUCLEAR ENERGY

About 250,000 Americans work in various nuclear energy industries. Many, but not all, are scientists and engineers. Most work for private industry, but a large number work for the federal government through the Department of Energy.

Uranium exploration and mining provide about 6,500 jobs. Most are for professionals such as geologists or mining engineers. Ore milling employs about 1,500 workers. These include repair personnel, pipe fitters, carpenters, electricians, and chemical process technicians, plus some scientists and engineers.

The uranium refining and enriching industry uses about 8,000 workers. Another 28,000 people work in the design and manufacture of nuclear reactors. Nearly half of these are scientists, engineers, and technicians. About 7,700 are involved in operating and maintaining nuclear reactors.

Nuclear scientists include physicists, chemists, mathematicians, biologists, and metallurgists. Engineering fields are nuclear, mechanical, electrical and electronic, chemical, metallurgical, and civil. Technicians include drafters, associates in engineering and physical sciences, and radiation monitors. Some of the most challenging nuclear work is in nuclear medicine. Nearly 8,000 people work in government nuclear energy offices around the country.

There are many different types of opportunities in the nuclear field. Education requirements range from completion of high school (with mathematics, chemistry, and physics) to advanced degrees from a college or university. Opportunities are expected to increase through the early nineties. Most jobs probably will be connected with electric power generation. Industrial and medical nuclear energy jobs also are expected to increase.

NUCLEAR
FUEL

Antoine Henri Becquerel detected uranium's radioactive properties more than 100 years after that element's discovery. Until the coming of the Nuclear Age, uranium often was used as a dye for pottery! These dyes range from yellow to dark green, and, by the way, they are radioactive enough to be used in simple radioactivity experiments.

The Nuclear Age caught the United States with only a tiny amount of uranium available. The uranium used in the World War II atomic bombs had to be imported from the Belgian Congo (now known as Zaire). After the war, the Atomic Energy Commission offered large bonuses as incentives for discovering uranium reserves in the United States.

Jeep-riding prospectors went on the hunt. They used Geiger counters that emitted telltale clicks in the presence of radioactivity. Some searchers became millionaires. ("Uraniumaires," they called themselves.) America's uranium deposits were found mostly in the Southwest, in Wyoming and the Four Corners region of Utah, Colorado, Arizona, and New Mexico. Large supplies of uranium also were found in Canada, Africa, and Australia.

Two kinds of uranium mining.
Above: *open pit;* right: *underground.*

Although a tiny amount of uranium holds thousands of times as much energy as coal, miners first must dig large amounts of raw ore. On the average, as we shall see, a ton of uranium ore yields only 5 pounds (2.3 kg) of uranium oxide. Some ore produces as little as 2 pounds (.9 kg) per ton. Thus the ore itself is not dangerous to handle. Uranium is mined mostly underground but sometimes from open pits. Underground mines must be carefully ventilated to get rid of radon gas present in the ore. Radon gas is dangerous to breathe and may cause lung cancer.

THE URANIUM ISOTOPES

Many elements can appear in nature in several different forms. First, there is the element's most common form. Then, there are its isotopes. These are identified by the number of neutrons in the atom. As you may recall, an element's number of protons and electrons never varies, but the number of neutrons can. When it does, you get isotopes.

You will soon read about **heavy water**, which is used in some nuclear reactors. Heavy water contains an isotope of hydrogen, called deuterium. The hydrogen atom present in normal water has a single proton in its nucleus, but no neutron. The hydrogen atom in heavy water does have a neutron along with its proton. The extra neutron in the isotope is what makes heavy water heavy. Another hydrogen isotope, tritium, has two neutrons with the normal proton.

Uranium comes in several isotope forms. More than 99 percent of the uranium mined is uranium 238. It has an **atomic weight** of 238. Atomic weight is the total number of protons and neutrons found in a single atom. Another isotope, uranium 235, composes less than 1 percent of all uranium mined. Uranium 235 is the isotope that readily fissions, or splits, when struck by neutrons. Although uranium 238 is not a practical fuel, it can be converted into a fissionable fuel, plutonium 239, by bombarding it with neutrons. (We shall say more about plutonium later.)

The element thorium is yet another radioactive fuel. When bombarded with neutrons, it becomes uranium 233, also a fissionable fuel.

MILLING

After mining, the next step is milling, or grinding the ore. This process produces uranium oxide, commonly known as "yellow cake." Many uranium mills operate in the United States. All of them are close to mining sites. It takes several steps to go from ore to cake. First, the ore is crushed. Then it is treated with chemicals to leach out, or dissolve, the uranium. Further chemical processes and a roasting treatment then remove the unwanted liquid. The resulting yellow cake is a concentrate that is about 70 to 90 percent uranium oxide. This product, representing a small fraction of the original ore, is then shipped to a refinery. There are only a few uranium refineries in the United States.

The refinery purifies the yellow cake, turning it into uranium tetrafluoride, more commonly called "green salt." The green salt is further purified to uranium hexafluoride, and enriched so that fission chain reaction can be kept up.

ENRICHMENT

Enriching uranium fuel means increasing the ratio of uranium 235 to uranium 238 in the mixture. *Gaseous diffusion*, a slow and expensive process, removes much of the uranium 238. It leaves the fissionable uranium 235. After enrichment, fuel contains about three times as much uranium 235 as uranium 238.

TRANSPORTING NUCLEAR FUEL AND OTHER RADIOACTIVE MATERIALS

Less than 1 percent of nuclear shipments contains fuel for power plants. The rest are weapons, medical equipment, and industrial

Above: *at a gaseous diffusion plant a worker is shown among the compressors, diffusers and pipes through which the uranium, in the form of a gas, is pumped to achieve enrichment.*
Right: *moving spent fuel. The container, holding four fuel assemblies, is a water-filled stainless steel cylinder, clad with four inches of metal shielding, enclosed by a shell of thick steel plate, surrounded by five inches of water, and held in a corrugated stainless steel outer jacket.*

material. The Nuclear Regulatory Commission and the Department of Transportation have set up rules for the movement of all nuclear materials.

Packaging must meet certain safety requirements. The material must be transported in a suitable vehicle. A small shipment of low-radiation material for medical or industrial use may be sent by mail or parcel delivery. Larger amounts and higher-radiation materials call for special packaging and handling. Shipments that include highly enriched nuclear fuel, which can be made into weapons, may be accompanied by armed guards.

Those who move nuclear materials take special care to protect the public and the environment. Nuclear fuel is very compact and does not involve as many vehicles or trips as the transportation of oil or gas. But accidents are bound to happen occasionally. Trucks carrying dangerous nuclear materials have overturned, and trains have derailed. But so far, no radiation has escaped. The nuclear industry feels that its safety record is far better than that for oil, gas, or even coal. We will explore this view later.

OUR NUCLEAR FUEL SUPPLY

Geologists estimate that each square mile (2.6 sq km) of the earth's crust down to a depth of 100 feet (30 m) contains, on the average, about 12,000 tons of uranium and thorium. You might think, therefore, that we would never run out of nuclear fuels. However, not all the ore can be mined. In many cases, it is too difficult or expensive to dig out and process.

About ten years ago, yellow cake sold for $5 a pound (.45 kg). The price increased dramatically. (At one point it was $50 a pound.) In 1983 it was about $25 a pound. The increase in price is simply explained. That uranium which was easiest and cheapest to mine has been used up. Five years ago some authorities feared that by the end of the century we would run out of the cheap uranium used in many of our present-day reactors. This seems less likely now, since the number of nuclear plants being built and contracted for has decreased.

Another way to look at the uranium supply is to look at another kind of reactor—the breeder reactor. As its name suggests, it manufactures, or "breeds," additional nuclear fuel. We will describe the breeder in a later chapter.

HOW A
NUCLEAR PLANT
OPERATES

The steam engine, invented several centuries ago, uses the steam from boiling water. Today, steam drives generators, which produce electricity to power machines and provide light and heat for homes and industries. Much of today's power still comes from steam. Even the most advanced nuclear power plants simply use nuclear fuel's energy to turn water into steam.

The nuclear reactor is the most important part of the nuclear power plant. It is the "container" where nuclear chain reactions are set into motion. Here are the basic parts of a reactor:

- a **core**, which contains the fuel.

- a **moderator**, a substance that acts to slow down the fast-moving neutrons to a speed likely to cause fission.

- **control rods** usually made of metal that absorbs excess neutrons. These control rods help prevent the chain reaction from "running away with itself," and just melting the uranium fuel

- **a coolant**, which carries heat away from the reactor to a boiler where steam is made.

- **shielding**, which prevents radiation from escaping into the environment.

THE CORE

Uranium is the most used fuel in today's reactors. Uranium pellets are put in metal tubes, made of stainless steel or zirconium. The tubes are then placed in the reactor's core. A coolant (see above) circulates around them.

Neutrons, freed by the fission of atomic nuclei move around in the core and cause the fission of more uranium atoms in a chain reaction. The chain reaction continues for a long time, producing heat energy. Eventually, however, used-up fuel builds up, and this waste product reduces the amount of heat given off. The core becomes something like a fireplace where ashes build up and, eventually, smother the fire. Then the nuclear waste, like the ashes, must be removed, and a new batch of nuclear fuel must be added.

THE MODERATOR

At first, neutrons from the fission of uranium fuel move very rapidly. Slower-moving neutrons are more likely to cause fission, so a moderating material to slow down neutrons is needed. The moderating material must slow down the neutrons without absorbing them. Otherwise, they could not bombard other neutrons and cause more fission.

Graphite (the material that is used in pencils) was the moderator for America's first nuclear reactor. It is still used in some reactors. But most of today's reactors use either ordinary water or heavy water (also called deuterium oxide). The hydrogen atoms in water have about the same mass as neutrons and thus make good moderating materials.

A NUCLEAR REACTOR

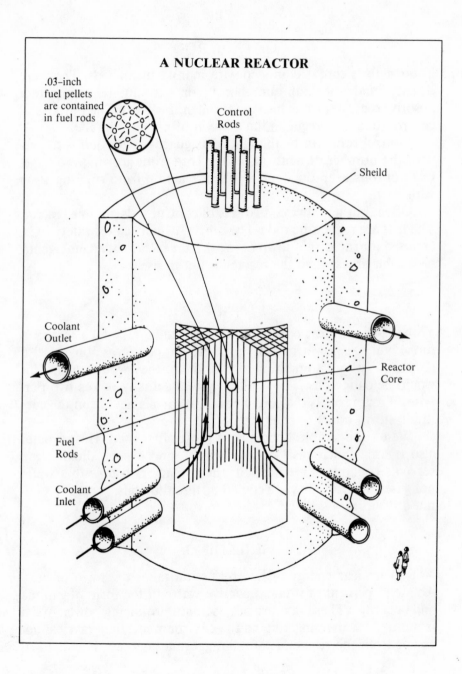

.03–inch fuel pellets are contained in fuel rods

Control Rods

Sheild

Coolant Outlet

Reactor Core

Fuel Rods

Coolant Inlet

CONTROL RODS

The reactor's core is equipped with many control rods. These are usually made of cadmium, boron, or hafnium (elements that absorb excess neutrons moving through the core). The purpose of control rods is to regulate the *amount* of heat produced.

Control rods can be thought of as guards. Their job is to prevent the number of neutrons in the core from growing too large. Control rods keep the neutron chain reaction from running away with itself.

Often, but not always, two sets of control rods are in a reactor. The first are regulating rods. The others, usually called safety rods, are used for rapid shutdown of the reactor in case of an emergency or for the times when the reactor is not in use.

COOLANT

To be efficient, heat engines must operate at very high temperatures. Nuclear power reactors produce temperatures above 500°F (260°C). Without something to cool them, they would melt. This would be dangerous. The cooling system actually serves two purposes. First, it cools the core. Second, it carries heat from the core to the steam boiler.

Water, the simplest coolant, is most often used. Heavy water also is used. Such gases as air, helium, and carbon dioxide can serve as coolants. The most advanced reactors use neither water nor gases. Instead, they are cooled by liquid metals, generally sodium or lithium.

SHIELDING

Not all nuclear energy caused by fission takes the form of heat. About 15 percent of it is radioactive waste in the form of gamma and beta rays. These rays are not useful in producing power. What is more, they are dangerous to the environment. Beta rays cannot escape from the reactor's core, but gamma rays can. For this reason, the entire reactor must be surrounded by shields that reduce the amount of escaping gamma radiation.

The nuclear reactor is housed in a specially constructed building called the **containment building**. It is topped by a reinforced concrete dome that serves as an outer shield. The very thick concrete has an inner lining of steel. This structure is designed to keep in the radioactive debris if there is a serious reactor accident. The modern reactor containment dome can survive great heat and pressure. It could survive even if a jet airliner happened to crash into it.

All nuclear reactors are designed to produce steam for turning generators that produce electricity. However there are several different types of reactors. These include pressurized water reactors (PWR), which use water as a coolant, high-temperature gas reactors (HTGR), which use helium gas as a coolant, and the breeder reactor (see Chapter 4), which is cooled with sodium or helium and uses plutonium as well as uranium for fuel.

The nuclear part of a nuclear power plant is much different from a power plant fueled with coal, oil, or gas. However, both plants use the same kind of steam-operated electric generators. Your TV set or toaster can't tell the difference between nuclear-generated and fossil-fuel-generated electricity.

PRESSURIZED-WATER REACTORS

Ordinary water, also referred to as "light water," is the most common form of coolant. The most common form of light-water reactor is the pressurized-water reactor (PWR). It was developed from the same system that runs the U.S. Navy nuclear-powered submarines. In this process, the water is subjected to extremely high pressure (approximately 2,200 pounds per square inch). Because it is under pressure, the water can absorb a lot of heat without turning to steam. The pressurized water, also referred to as the primary

Left: *looking into the core of a nuclear
reactor.* Above: *worm's eye view of a reactor
vessel being lowered into the containment building.*

coolant, must keep flowing through the reactor. Otherwise the water would overheat. Massive pumps (9,000 horsepower each) push this primary coolant up through the uranium core. From there, it is carried by large pipes (1 yard, or .9 m, in diameter) to steel tanks—the steam generators. Other water (not under pressure), known as the secondary cooling water or secondary coolant, gets to the same steel tanks by means of feedwater pumps.

The primary coolant and the secondary coolant do not actually mix in the steam generators. As it comes from the reactor, the primary coolant—now very hot—is fed into thousands of small tubes in the generator. These tubes are surrounded by the secondary coolant. The heat is transferred to the secondary cooling water, which in turn boils and is transformed into steam. From there the process resembles what happens at fossil-fuel power plants. The steam goes into a turbine, which is attached to an electric generator. The steam causes the turbine blades to spin, which causes the generator to spin. The generator's motion creates an electric current.

THE SELECTION OF
A NUCLEAR
POWER PLANT SITE

Nuclear power plants cannot be built just anywhere. Like other power plants, they should be built near large cities so that the electricity won't have to be carried long distances. But a nuclear power plant must not be built *too* near a large city. Furthermore, before such a plant may be built, the builder must present an evacuation plan that is approved by regulatory agencies. Such a plan must give all the details of how the people who live within 10 miles (16 km) of the plant would get out of the area quickly in an emergency.

In some ways, it is easier to site a nuclear power plant than a fossil-fuel power plant. For example, a coal-fired power plant may require thirty railroad cars of coal every day. A nuclear plant can go a year on just one truckload of uranium fuel! Thus, it is not necessary to build a nuclear plant near its fuel supply. It often is necessary to do so with fossil-fuel plants.

Nuclear power plants are clean, quiet, and streamlined in design. Coal-run power plants produce air pollution and are usually unattractive too.

However, there are some important restrictions on selecting a nuclear power plant site. It should not, for example, be built on earthquake-prone territory. A quake might damage the reactor and release radioactive materials into the environment. Water-cooled nuclear plants must be near a large amount of cooling water. And what seems to be the most appropriate site may be challenged. People may oppose the placement of a nuclear power site near where they live. Some people are afraid because they don't know how nuclear power plants work, and some people are afraid because they do.

THE BREEDER
REACTOR

The **breeder reactor** is designed to save fuel. It uses plutonium and uranium 238 as its fuel and is not equipped with a moderator to slow down neutrons. For this reason, it sometimes is called a "fast breeder." The reactor produces power by fissioning the plutonium. During the process, neutrons also strike the uranium, converting it to plutonium. That plutonium, "reprocessed," can be used as fuel once more. In time a breeder reactor can "breed" or make more usable fuel than it started out with, not only for its own operation, but also for another reactor.

FUEL EFFICIENCY

Does this mean the breeder produces fuel out of nothing? Not quite! The breeder uses and reuses the same fuel, each time extracting a little more of the fuel's energy. Eventually all the original fuel will be used up. But breeder reactors also can be operated on "tailings," the waste uranium from light-water reactors.

The breeder reactor may permit the use of as much as 50 percent of uranium's energy instead of the 1 percent or less used by light-water reactors. This would extend the life of our uranium supplies by about 5,000 percent.

"Doubling time" is the time it takes for one breeder reactor to produce enough plutonium fuel to operate another reactor. Nuclear engineers hope to achieve doubling times as short as ten years.

Instead of water, breeder reactors usually are cooled with a liquid metal such as sodium or a gas such as helium. These can absorb more heat than other coolants, and thus the reactor is more efficient. This not only saves money in fuel, but is also safer environmentally. Since more of the breeder reactor's heat goes to making steam, less is wasted by escaping to the outside world. Thus, breeder reactors do not heat up the environment as much as light-water reactors do.

HALTING THE
BREEDER PROGRAM

The first breeder reactor (Experimental Breeder Reactor I) was operated in the United States in 1951 at an Idaho nuclear research center. The U.S. government's Experimental Breeder Reactor II has operated successfully since 1964 at the same place. The government planned to have the Clinch River Fast Breeder (near Oak Ridge, Tennessee) operating in the 1980s. But President Carter halted its development and called on other governments to do the same.

President Carter feared that plutonium produced by a reactor could fall into the hands of terrorists or foreign agents. While uranium is not sufficiently enriched to be suitable for making atom

The French Superphénix
Breeder reactor, scheduled
to go on line in 1984.

bombs, plutonium is. Just a few pounds would enable somebody to make a powerful weapon. Carter felt that as more countries become nuclear powers, the danger of nuclear war or nuclear terrorism increased.

President Reagan, Carter's successor, held a different view of breeder reactors and the Clinch River Project. Reagan felt that the United States should continue experimenting with breeder reactors. His first budget allocated *more* funds for Clinch River. The Clinch River battle was full of suspense. Contradictory views were expressed within the Nuclear Regulatory Commission, the Congress, and the courts. In June of 1983, both houses of Congress voted to withhold funding for Clinch River. It seemed that the project, once again was abandoned, although the Clinch River Project has shown a remarkable ability to survive.

Despite America's concern, France, the United Kingdom, the Soviet Union, Germany, and Japan have begun to operate breeder reactors. These nations do not have abundant coal resources as we do. They fear that lack of resources could destroy their way of life and perhaps plunge them into another Dark Age.

France leads other nations in this work. France's Phoenix breeder, with an output of about 250 megawatts, has been operating for several years. Now France is building the Superphoenix, a larger breeder reactor with an electric output of about 1,200 megawatts. The breeder reactor's future is not clear. Other heads of state may feel as Carter did. And additional problems face all nuclear power plants. We shall take these up in the next chapter.

THE DANGERS OF NUCLEAR ENERGY

Despite its great energy potential, nuclear power is a controversial public issue. For several years, nuclear power's expansion has been slowed by the determined action of individuals and organizations. Here and abroad, demonstrations, the picketing of construction sites, pressure on elected officials, and lawsuits seeking to shut down nuclear plants all have played a role. Those who oppose nuclear power plant construction say that atomic reactors will provide something other than energy—namely, sickness, death, and disaster. Why do they feel this way?

As we know, hundreds of thousands of Japanese were killed or maimed by the two 1945 atom bombs. Most of the deaths resulted from the blast and heat of the explosions. This cannot happen with a reactor because there is not enough enriched uranium present to make a nuclear blast possible. However, many of the victims suffered radiation sickness, cancer, and other long-term effects of overexposure to radiation. These are the problems that could be caused by a serious nuclear plant accident.

Marie Curie and her daughter both died of leukemia, cancer of the blood, induced by exposure to radiation from radium. Many factory workers who painted radium on watch dials to make the

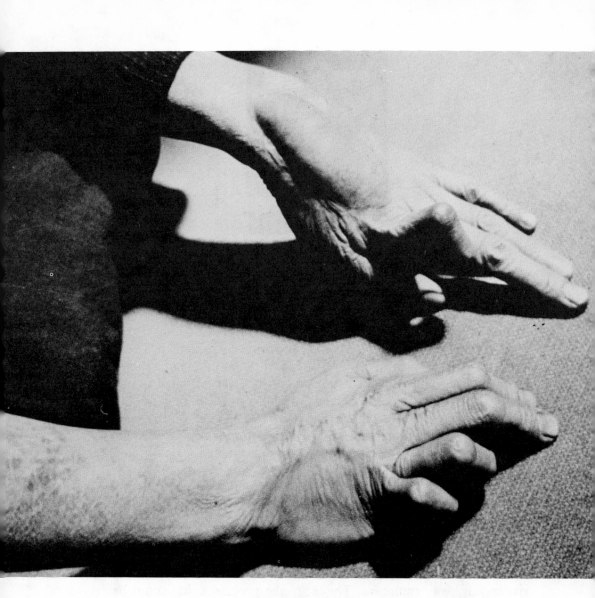

Results of radiation poisoning show in the hands of this Hiroshima victim.

dials glow at night died from radiation exposure. A twelve-year-long British study (1953–1965) indicated a larger than average number of cancer cases in children whose mothers were exposed to radiation in the form of X rays. In 1954, the crew of a Japanese fishing boat, ironically named *Lucky Dragon*, was showered with radioactive fallout from an American nuclear test. The crew suffered radiation sickness.

A number of scientists estimate that every year tens of thousands of people are harmed by atomic testing and nuclear power plant operation. They also worry about radiation from nuclear wastes. Nuclear power plants are not the only cause of such damage, however. Most of the man-made radiation now in the environment has come from the explosion of atom bombs or other test devices. Nuclear plants contribute only a small fraction. In fact, "background" radiation from cosmic rays and natural materials far exceeds that produced by nuclear power plants.

HEAT POLLUTION

There is also a hazard to the environment from waste heat. About two-thirds of the heat energy generated by a light-water nuclear power plant is wasted, and heats the air or water around it. It can make the surrounding environment too warm for the creatures and plants that inhabit the area. This "heat pollution" concerns environmentalists and nuclear engineers alike. We must make sure it does not harm living creatures and plants—including our food.

It's possible that some waste heat might be put to good use. Experiments to this end are being conducted in agriculture and aquaculture (the farming of marine life).

THE RISK OF
NUCLEAR CATASTROPHE

The government has sponsored many studies concerning nuclear risks. One frequently cited 1975 study suggested the possibility of a nuclear accident once every 200 years. It estimated that there is as much chance of being killed in a nuclear accident as there is of being struck by lightning. It added that the chance of a nuclear catastrophe's killing a large number of people was no greater than that of a meteor's hitting a populated region of the earth.

However, people continued to wonder. What if the unlikely *did* happen? Suppose a nuclear plant should break down? Or be destroyed by saboteurs? Or be damaged in such natural occurrences as an earthquake, hurricane, or flood? A government study of a nuclear catastrophe's worst possible consequences estimated that a full-scale nuclear reactor accident would cause tens of thousands of deaths. The disaster area, according to the study, would equal the size of the state of Pennsylvania.

A movie called *The China Syndrome* opened in March 1979. It centered on the possibility of an accident at a nuclear plant. The "China syndrome" is a phrase some nuclear workers use to describe a theoretical situation called a **meltdown.** If the cooling system failed and the temperature in the reactor rose to 5,000°F (2,760°C), the hot uranium would begin to melt. The nuclear core, a mass of melted radioactive metal, would then drop through its steel housing. At this point, a series of drastic events would occur. There would be explosions (not nuclear explosions, but dangerous nonetheless). And, much worse, large amounts of radioactive materials would be released into the atmosphere. A meltdown was dubbed "the China syndrome" as a grim joke; theoretically, the hot radioactive core might burn its way right through the earth to China.

The movie—which starred Michael Douglas, Jane Fonda, and Jack Lemmon—was about a power plant that experienced a Loss Of Coolant Accident, or LOCA. (A LOCA happens when something prevents the needed amount of coolant from circulating around the nuclear core.) Although most critics liked the film, some considered it "farfetched" and "misleading." Such comments were stilled two weeks later.

In fact, *all* discussions of nuclear catastrophe fall into two categories—everything said before March 28, 1979, and everything said afterward. On that date, nuclear debaters shifted their focus from theories developed in laboratories to the real-life drama taking place at the Three Mile Island Nuclear Energy Plant Unit 2 near Harrisburg, Pennsylvania.

THREE MILE
ISLAND

In the early morning on March 28, 1979, a pump in a nuclear reactor failed to work. This malfunction started a chain of events that focused world attention on Three Mile Island. Both those who favor and those who oppose the use of nuclear power feel that the Three Mile Island accident can teach us something important. However, the two camps have learned two different lessons. We can understand why by looking at what happened.

At 4 a.m., a feedwater pump, which carries water to the nuclear power plant's steam generators, stopped operating. This occurs every so often at nuclear power plants. When it happens, the control rods are supposed to drop very quickly into the uranium core. This process, known as "scramming," stops the chain reaction. The reactor did scram at Three Mile Island; backup pumps should then have started to feed water into the system. The backup feedwater pumps were not connected. Their valves which, when open, allow water to pass through, were closed. Usually the water serving as primary coolant travels from the core to the steam generators and back. Because the backup pump valves were closed, there was no water for the steam generators to boil. Furthermore, the prima-

ry coolant water could not flow away from the nuclear core. This was important because although the chain reaction (which causes neutrons to bombard other neutrons) stopped, the natural atomic fission (the release of neutrons) continued. The nuclear pile's decay gave off heat that rapidly sent the coolant's temperature up. The blistering temperatures turned the trapped coolant into steam. At this point, a safety valve blew open—standard procedure to relieve pressure.

AN OPEN VALVE

Having relieved the pressure, the valve should have closed immediately. Instead, it remained open. But the operators in the Three Mile Island control room were not aware of the open valve. For two hours the valve allowed radioactive water to drain slowly from the reactor system and onto the floor of the containment building. Now, there was not enough water flowing around the reactor, and too much water was on the containment building floor. Pumps "efficiently" sent the contaminated water into radioactive-waste storage tanks in the auxiliary building, which was connected to the containment building. These tanks quickly overflowed. Meanwhile the hot decay continued to create steam.

In the Three Mile Island control room, workers were striving to return the situation to normal. They did not know about the water that was being emptied out. The control room contained 600 alarm lights and more than 1,000 different dials, gauges, and switch indi-

Three Mile Island, where reactor number two (left foreground) was shut down because of failure of its cooling pump. The massive containment domes look small next to the four huge cooling towers.

cators. Against a background of flashing lights and loud alarms, the workers examined the instrument readings and made all the adjustments that seemed called for. Unfortunately, some instrument readings were providing inaccurate information.

According to the control panel, the water level at the uranium core was too high. Actually, it was too low. Meanwhile the system itself had reacted to the lack of water and automatically turned on the pumps of the Emergency Core Cooling System (ECCS). The ECCS is an emergency supply of cooling water designed to be rushed into the core area. The men in the control room however reacted to the false reading and turned off the ECCS.

At approximately 4:10 a.m. the operators discovered that the backup feedwater pump valves were stuck. They immediately opened the valves and activated the pumps. The next hour was spent in trying to balance the flow of water according to instrument readings. However, the people in the control room did not realize that the pressure-relief valve still was open. Water that should have been cooling the reactor was leaving the core and leaking into the containment building.

THE CORE'S
TEMPERATURE RISES

Sometime after 5 a.m. a new round of alarms and flashing lights startled the crew. The new alerts signaled that the coolant pumps, which are two stories high, were shaking. The problem was that they were designed to deliver only water and instead they were pumping a mixture of water and steam. At first, the operators thought a leaky steam generator was responsible. The control panel's alarms, lights, and readings gave no clue that the operators could read. Fire alarms began to clang and operators thought that somehow the chain reaction, which had been shut down, was starting again. Actually the instruments were thrown into confusion by the presence of steam where no steam ought to be.

Since the operators wished to stop the chain reaction they mistakenly thought was taking place, they went to the next official step—stopping a chain reaction by means of an *emergency boration*. They introduced *boron*, a chemical, to the core. Boron serves the same purpose as control rods in that it absorbs neutrons.

The core temperatures continued to climb. (Normally the temperature is about 600°F, or 315°C. At this point, it was about 4,000°F, or 2,200°C). By 6 a.m. the Zircaloy (zirconium alloy) fuel rods holding the uranium pellets began to burn. A chemical reaction between the Zircaloy and steam began to take place. The two combined to form zirconium dioxide. Hydrogen gas was a by-product. The operators did not know this was happening.

At 6:18 a.m., a man just reporting to work correctly guessed that a pressure valve was open and should be closed. However, nobody realized how much water had been lost, and therefore the emergency cooling system was not turned back on. At about 6:45 a.m. alarms announced that there were high radiation levels in the plant. Civilian authorities were called. They included Dauphin County Civil Defense; Pennsylvania's governor, Richard Thornburgh; the Nuclear Regulatory Commission; and the president of the United States, Jimmy Carter.

A SERIOUS SITUATION

In the hours that followed a number of startling facts became evident.

The nuclear core, which is to be shielded at all times, was partially exposed as the Zircaloy melted away. If the temperature continued to increase, the core would undergo a meltdown. The chilling events of the movie *The China Syndrome* threatened to become a dangerous reality.

Some radioactive gas had been released from the auxiliary building. Radiation in the containment building had long since exceeded the danger levels. (People within the power plant had to

wear protective clothing even in areas where they normally wore ordinary clothes.)

A bubble of hydrogen gas was growing between the dome and the uranium core. This inspired two fears. First, as long as the hydrogen bubble remained, it would interfere with efforts to cool the system down. Second, if the hydrogen combined with enough oxygen (nine parts of hydrogen to one part of oxygen), an explosion would result. It would not be a nuclear explosion (in which atoms are either split or fused), but it would be damaging. And it probably would release large amounts of radiation into the atmosphere.

Experts gathered from around the country. At about 7:30 p.m., approximately fifteen hours after the event began, a pump was started that sent cooling water past the core, averting disaster. Some experts claim Three Mile Island was thirty minutes to an hour away from a meltdown.

The problem of the hydrogen bubble remained. The gathered workers monitored the bubble to keep track of its size. After three days, it became apparent that the hydrogen would not explode. There simply was not enough oxygen present. (Later it was discovered that there had actually been a small hydrogen explosion earlier. This may have used enough oxygen to make a later explosion impossible.) Without the danger of explosion to worry about, a plan was developed to reduce the amount of hydrogen gas. Using very ordinary technologies, the workers drained the hydrogen from the containment building. By Sunday, four days after the Three Mile Island accident began, the hydrogen bubble was gone.

For the first time since the incident, engineers enter the airlock leading to the reactor building at the Three Mile Island nuclear plant. This was almost a year after the event.

The Three Mile Island accident, described as the worst nuclear occurrence in United States history, was over. By the time it ended, 144,000 people had fled the surrounding area. It is estimated that this unofficial evacuation plus the wages lost by people who could not get to work amounted to $18.2 million. Current estimates put the Three Mile Island cleanup at about $975 million. This monumental job probably will not be finished until 1988.

AFTER
THREE MILE
ISLAND

A catastrophe was avoided at Three Mile Island, but conditions did not return to normal. The plant is still shut down. The level of radioactivity within the unit still exceeds safety standards. Thousands of gallons of radioactive water still have to be removed. On the positive side, despite the near disaster, not a single person died as a result.

Many investigations of the Three Mile Island accident were launched. Among the most frustrating of discoveries was the simple fact that this accident could have been avoided. After checking a Chicago power plant, a Nuclear Regulatory Commission inspector foresaw the possibility of such a problem. He recommended a procedure to follow in the event of stuck valves. His memo had been ignored. Now, of course, people were willing to pay attention.

Investigators also turned their attention to the Three Mile Island control room. The general feeling was that the massive array of controls, lights, and switches was not arranged in an intelligent

*The control room of a nuclear plant has
a bewildering array of lights and switches.*

easy-to-understand fashion. In fact, the control panel was confusing and difficult to work with.

In addition, a lot of thought went to the procedures by which power companies earned the right to build and operate nuclear plants. It had always been assumed that power companies and manufacturers of equipment would correct potential problems—if only out of self-interest. This turned out to be a false assumption. Now the federal government is setting stricter standards. The goal is to resolve potential problems before a nuclear plant goes into operation. The government is also being stricter about seeing to it that power companies keep their nuclear systems in good repair. And people who work in nuclear power plants are getting more and better training in how to handle emergencies.

Who was responsible for the Three Mile Island incident? The company that built the reactor? The company that designed the reactor? The company that owned and operated the Three Mile Island power plant? Or the Nuclear Regulatory Commission? (As it happens, the owner sued the builder and got a favorable out-of-court settlement.) But clearly, no one group bears all the blame.

THE LESSONS

The Pennsylvania accident did not help to clarify the role of atomic energy in our future.

Opponents of nuclear power assert that the Three Mile Island accident shows how vulnerable we are to a power plant mishap. They say that the combination of faulty equipment and human error easily could happen again. The next time, they warn, the results might be devastating.

Those who favor atomic power argue just the opposite. They say that the Three Mile Island incident showed up the areas of weakness and this will help us improve both present and future atomic power plants. They feel that the elaborate series of safety procedures did work, and can be made to work even better. Finally, they point out that, despite all the tension and drama, there were no deaths or injuries.

PROTESTS

Before Three Mile Island, there had been many small, if determined, protests against the use of nuclear energy. The Pennsylvania accident, however, gave rise to demonstrations around the world. In Hanover, Germany, nearly 50,000 people gathered to object to the building of a nuclear power plant near that community. They chanted, "We all live in Pennsylvania." A French mayor was held captive for a few hours by residents of his town. They disagreed with his pronuclear stand. Although no nuclear power plants were to be found in Denmark, Danish people protested plants that were in nearby areas of Sweden.

Of course, there were demonstrations in the United States. On May 6, 1979, close to 70,000 people assembled in Washington, D.C. This had been the largest American protest to date against the use of nuclear energy. The speakers included consumer advocate Ralph Nader, California governor Edmund G. ("Jerry") Brown, actress Jane Fonda, and political activist Tom Hayden (later elected to the California legislature). This demonstration was dwarfed by one held more than four months later in New York City. On September 23, 200,000 people turned out to demonstrate. A number of popular musicians organized this event. In addition to hearing speeches by Nader, Hayden, and Fonda, the crowds were entertained by such musicians as Jackson Browne, Graham Nash, Bonnie Raitt, and Pete Seeger.

NUCLEAR REGULATION:
THE SILKWOOD CASE

"Three Mile Island" and "The China Syndrome" were phrases that had deep and powerful meanings, especially for the antinuclear forces. To these phrases, a name was added—"Silkwood." It did

*The problems at Three Mile Island triggered
protests against the use of nuclear power.*

not stand for a place or event. It was the name of a person—Karen Silkwood. Great controversy involving the nuclear industry swirled around her life and death. (She, too, is the subject of a film, *Silkwood*, released at the end of 1983.) A vital issue in the Silkwood case concerns nuclear regulation.

Karen Silkwood worked at Kerr-McGee's Cimarron, Oklahoma, uranium processing plant. Kerr-McGee was a major supplier of uranium fuel to power plants. Karen Silkwood, a laboratory analyst, began to feel that safety procedures at the Cimarron plant were inadequate. She also claimed that she was becoming contaminated by plutonium, to which she was exposed at the plant. One of the people to whom she complained was a reporter for *The New York Times*. In 1974, Karen Silkwood had an appointment with the newspaperman. He had come to her community so that she could show him evidence of her charges. She never made the meeting. She died alone in a car crash on her way.

After Karen Silkwood's death, Kerr-McGee was sued on behalf of her family. The suit had nothing to do with the way in which she died. Kerr-McGee was accused of not being careful enough with the radioactive materials, thereby causing her to be contaminated by plutonium. The first trial took place in 1979, lasting for close to three months. There was a key issue for the jury to decide: According to Oklahoma law, were Kerr-McGee's safety procedures to blame? The company's lawyers suggested that Karen Silkwood stole plutonium and thereby contaminated herself.

The jury listened to the testimony of forty-five witnesses and studied hundreds of exhibits before reaching a verdict. The jury decided that Kerr-McGee was responsible for Karen Silkwood's excessive exposure to plutonium. Furthermore, the jury ruled that Kerr-McGee, as punishment for negligence, had to pay $10,000,000 to Karen Silkwood's survivors.

But the Silkwood case was not over. Its twists and turns went beyond the question of what happened to Karen Silkwood. At issue was the continuing battle over which aspects of nuclear power are to be regulated by state governments and which by the federal government. The argument goes like this: nuclear safety is regulated by the federal government. With this in mind, to what extent may the states make up their own regulations about atomic energy?

The Silkwood verdict was appealed by Kerr-McGee. This time the appeals court ruled that using Oklahoma's law about negligence (carelessness that leads to accidents) was really a way of allowing the state to regulate nuclear safety, which is supposed to be federally regulated. The appeals court ruled that Kerr-McGee did not have to pay the $10,000,000 fine.

Again the case was appealed. This time the case went to the Supreme Court. Again, the outcome had broader significance than its effect on Kerr-McGee or Karen Silkwood's family. It was going to affect how much control individual states could have over nuclear power within their borders. More than a dozen states filed arguments in support of the Silkwood claim.

The Supreme Court's nine judges listened to the evidence very carefully. They offered no final opinion as to whether the Silkwood or Kerr-McGee side was right about whether there had been negligence. Instead, in a close decision (5–4), the Supreme Court said that although a state court's awarding damages in a negligence case, was a form of regulation, it did not interfere with federal rights and was permissible. Therefore, the Supreme Court ruled, the federal appeals court would have to take another look at the case. That was early 1984. At the time of this writing, the lower court had not yet reached a new verdict. You can be sure that, regardless of the court's decision, the name "Silkwood" will symbolize controversy.

NUCLEAR REGULATION
OF SAFETY

Four of the Supreme Court judges in the Silkwood case were concerned lest state regulations conflict with the basic idea of overall federal regulation of nuclear safety. The Nuclear Regulatory Com-

mission (NRC) is supposed to keep track of nuclear safety throughout the country. Each time a problem is found in one nuclear plant, the NRC alerts other plants that may suffer from the same condition. These may be plants that use the same troublesome material in similar trouble spots; or they may have been built by the same construction companies; or they may have bought the same parts from the same suppliers. For example, in early 1984 a crack was found in a steam pipe in a shut-down plant in Baxley, Georgia. The NRC instructed five other plants with similar reactors to check their steam pipes.

An example of potentially troublesome material is steel. Approximately twenty of the country's reactors use a kind of steel known as "high-strength steel" to shield their containment domes. This steel withstands weight and stress better than ordinary steel. However, it is not as flexible and is proving to be unexpectedly brittle. It is possible that cracks could develop in containment dome shielding. Such a development would be dangerous. So, the power companies that use high-strength steel are checking the shielding very carefully. One company, Carolina Power & Light, is constructing a special extra shield around its high-strength steel walls. Other companies may have to do the same.

In the post–Three Mile Island period, events and circumstances seem to conspire against nuclear power.

DELAYED CONSTRUCTION

The Nuclear Regulatory Commission, taking a more active approach, has delayed the licensing of some reactors and ordered the shutdown of others for repairs. For example, in 1981 the NRC suspended the preliminary license of the Diablo Canyon plant in

There are also demonstrations for nuclear power. Strong arguments exist on both sides.

Avila Beach, California. The commission cited thirteen design and construction errors. In March 1982, more than 100 additional definite and possible errors were identified at the Diablo Canyon site, further delaying the plant's opening. This is particularly worth noting as Avila Beach lies right in the heart of earthquake territory!

In late 1982, the NRC made detailed inspections of construction sites in Texas, Indiana, and Ohio. The NRC called a halt to the construction of the Ohio plant, the William Zimmer–1 reactor, even though more than 95 percent of the construction work was completed. In 1984, the Cincinnati Gas and Electric Company decided to convert its Zimmer project to coal.

In early 1984, the nuclear energy industry received another shock. The NRC refused to permit a nearly completed nuclear power plant in the Chicago area to start operating. This permission, which comes in the form of granting a license, can be withheld until certain safety conditions are satisfied. In this case, Commonwealth Edison of Chicago was not even given the option of making changes in its Byron Nuclear Power Station located near Rockford, Illinois. Although the Byron plant had cost more than $3.5 billion to build, the NRC explained that it had no confidence that the plant could operate safely, even if changes were made. This was the very first time the NRC has ever denied a license unconditionally.

Construction delays and rigorous safety requirements have made it extremely costly to build nuclear power plants. In 1983 the Long Island Lighting Company (LILCO) discovered cracks in each of the three crankshafts in the diesel generators at its new Shoreham nuclear plant. Company officials estimated that delays in opening the plant would cost LILCO about $40 million per month. Nuclear power no longer seemed to be such a bargain.

THE ENERGY CRISIS
OF 1973

The big push to turn to nuclear power as a source of electricity came in the late 1960s and early 1970s. In 1973 the world experienced an oil shortage. Many of the countries that produced and sold oil limited the amount of oil they were willing to sell. This "oil embargo" immediately made oil more expensive. It also made many countries, including the United States, realize how dependent they were on oil. We worried about how much oil the producing countries were willing to sell to us. Would they withhold oil if they didn't like our foreign policies? What would happen if an oil-producer's government were overthrown?

Another consideration had nothing to do with politics. There is only so much oil in the ground. At a certain point, it will be gone. Then what shall we do?

In 1973, nuclear power seemed to be the answer. Building nuclear plants from scratch would cost a lot of money. But it might be cheaper in the long run than continued dependence on oil and coal. This kind of reasoning helped to increase interest in nuclear power.

However, an interest in nuclear power was not the oil embargo's only effect. Many people turned to energy conservation. People examined their lives and found ways to reduce the amount of energy they used. They installed light bulbs that used less power. They turned off lights in empty rooms, houses, and even tall skyscrapers. In the summertime, people carefully regulated their air-conditioning units. They insulated their houses so that less heat would escape in the winter and less oil would be used. They turned from large, gas-guzzling cars to smaller, more fuel-efficient ones. The result was that the oil-producing countries were left with a surplus of oil. Oil prices came down. However, people had learned to conserve energy. Even with oil once more available, the demand for it did not soar, so the prices stayed down.

While the cost of oil was going down, the cost of nuclear power, with all its expensive delays, was going up. Plans to build new reactors were canceled in many places. Nuclear opponents say that what all their arguments could not accomplish will be brought about by the simple economics of the situation. Atomic power plants now seem to cost too much to build and run. Those who favor the use of atomic energy are discouraged. They point out,

The Wrigley Building,
a blazing landmark in Chicago, was darkened
for the duration of the energy crisis.

however, that the realities of the oil crisis have not disappeared. The world's oil supply still is being depleted. The amount of oil we can buy from oil-producing countries still is dependent on international politics. Meanwhile, they argue, the safety problems of nuclear plants are being dealt with. They see only one other serious issue—radioactive waste.

RADIOACTIVE
WASTE

Even if all nuclear plants came to a halt today, we still would face a very serious problem. What are we to do with all the radioactive waste? Radioactive waste material consists of used-up nuclear fuel, contaminated water, and disposable items such as clothing and implements that have been exposed to radiation. The major concern is how to deal with the fuel and water. The rays emitted by radioactive waste are so dangerous that the waste cannot be treated in the same manner as ordinary debris. The waste must be put in safe, shielded locations for a very long time.

There are three forms of radiation—alpha, beta, and gamma rays. Gamma radiation is the most harmful. Exposure to gamma rays can have serious effects on living tissue, particularly the reproductive organs. Thus, gamma rays can harm not only the original victims, but also their offspring. Alpha and beta rays also can harm body cells. For example, they can cause various forms of cancer if they are inhaled or taken into the body through food.

In a nuclear reactor, uranium fuel yields its energy rapidly. In nature, the process of radioactive decay takes place very slowly; the unit of measurement is the "half-life." That's the length of time it takes for half the mass of a radioactive substance to decay into

A rail-mounted transfer vehicle was used to place canisters of spent fuel in storage holes in a testing program for the storage of nuclear waste.

another element. In its second half-life, only half of what is left decays, and so on. Each radioactive element has its own half-life. The half-life of uranium 235 is 710 million years! Plutonium's half-life is 24,360 years. An estimated 10 half-lives must pass before a radioactive material is absolutely safe. Any given amount of radioactive plutonium would not be considered harmless until 243,600 years had elapsed. Thus, radioactive waste will be a hazard for a very long time.

Actually, so far, few people have died of exposure to radiation from nuclear power plants. In fact, nuclear advocates claim that far more people die as a result of the air pollution caused by coal-fired power plants. However, we must resolve the nuclear waste disposal problem soon. It would be unfair to coming generations to leave them this kind of "buried treasure."

Early in the Nuclear Age, some radioactive wastes were sealed in steel drums or tanks and dumped in the ocean. Some time later the containers were found to be leaking, and this method was discarded as unsafe. It became apparent that more thought was required.

Basically, we can do only three things with nuclear waste: we can try to dispose of it permanently, we can store it temporarily, or we can reprocess it to recover more fuel for use in other nuclear reactors.

WASTE DISPOSAL

Over the years, a number of fantastic suggestions have been considered. One school of thought would have us put nuclear waste into a rocket and give it a one-way ride into outer space. This would be a very expensive way of "taking out the garbage." Furthermore, should there be a miscalculation or an accident at launch, a lot of dangerous radioactive material would be in the wrong place. This proposal may seem farfetched, but it shows how serious the experts are about keeping radioactive material away from people.

Another idea is to send the waste down 20,000-foot (6,100-m) holes that would be drilled in the earth. According to this theory, the hot nuclear material would melt the rock around it. The rock would later harden and keep the waste permanently sealed in. There is some question as to how these holes, which would have to be wide as well as deep, really could be drilled. Furthermore, U.S. government policy requires that stored radioactive waste be recoverable for approximately fifty years. Then, if something goes wrong in the waste site, the waste can be removed. But if rocks did solidify around the waste buried deep in the earth, the waste could not be recovered.

Other ideas include embedding the waste beneath the vast Antarctic ice sheets, or burying it beneath an ocean floor's rock sediments. But not enough is known about these environments to be sure that these measures would be safe.

SALTING WASTE AWAY

Some experts feel that "glassification" is a simple solution to nuclear waste. First, the waste would be turned into glass, by combining it with larger quantities of glass or ceramic. Then, it would be put into stainless steel containers. Both the steel and the glassification would keep the waste from leaking. The canisters then would be buried in subterranean salt deposits. Any holes that would be drilled would be refilled with rock.

Salt caverns are recommended for two reasons. First, there is no water in them. (If radioactive waste leaked into water, the water would spread it farther.) Second, salt is a good conductor of heat. It would carry the heat away from the waste more quickly than many other materials. But critics feel that over the hundreds of thousands of years of storage, geological formations might change and bring water to the storage area. They also fear that miners seeking other materials might someday bring the contaminated waste to the surface. Some people wonder whether any kind of accessible storage is wise. No one can guarantee who will be in control of the waste many thousands of years in the future. Perhaps a future government or individual would seize the radioactive waste and create the kind of disaster we are trying so hard to avoid.

REPROCESSING

Recycling (or "reprocessing") nuclear waste would seem to make disposal simpler as well. First, the waste would be taken to a special plant where uranium and plutonium would be retrieved. Obviously, there still would be waste. But with the uranium and plutonium removed, the remaining waste would be radioactive for a shorter period of time. Two serious obstacles impede such reprocessing.

Reprocessing is complex, difficult, and expensive. It's economical only if it's done on a very large scale. In order for a reprocessing plant to pay its way, the country would have to have a great many more reactors than are currently operating. Reprocessing's other problem is as real and immediate as today's headlines. The plutonium produced by this process could do more than light people's homes; it could also be the main ingredient in an atomic bomb, making it a prime target for terrorists or political extremists.

Citing these dangers, President Carter halted reprocessing. President Reagan reversed that order in 1981. However, none of the three commercial reprocessing plants started operations—nor are they operating now.

The waste disposal question has not been resolved, and nuclear waste continues to pile up at reactor sites around the country. The hot, radioactive waste is stored in pools of water kept in the auxiliary buildings. Boron is added to prevent the possibility of a nuclear reaction. In the course of a year approximately one-third of a reactor's nuclear fuel is used up and becomes radioactive waste. Time and space are running out.

The Carter administration tried to introduce temporary, safe *Away From Reactor* sites (AFRs). These would be like the storage pools at nuclear plants, but they would be larger, and centrally located so as to hold the waste from many reactors. Each would be the size of an average warehouse, and together they could provide adequate temporary storage for all the nuclear waste created until the end of the twentieth century.

This idea was greeted with hostility. Local governments (state, county, and city) did not want radioactive waste within their borders. California outlawed nuclear plants in that state until a technology for nuclear waste disposal proved effective. This law was upheld by the Supreme Court.

TRANSPORTATION

The outcry against AFRs highlighted one more problem. Just how would radioactive waste travel from a plant to temporary storage or final disposal sites? People are understandably upset about the prospect of large quantities of radioactive material traveling through their streets and past their homes. Nearly 250 state and local governments have passed laws saying if, when, and how nuclear waste may be moved through their communities. The problem is complicated by the increasing amount of nuclear waste. In the early 1980s, about ninety-five shipments of radioactive waste material were transported in a year. It is estimated that by the year 2000, that figure will have climbed to 120 shipments a day.

Successful test crash. A 22-ton shipping cask for spent nuclear fuel was mounted on a tractor-trailer rig and propelled by rockets into a concrete target at 84 mph. The cask was deformed but not breached or broken.

At the end of 1982, Congress passed the Nuclear Waste Policy Act of 1982. According to this law, signed by President Reagan, the United States government takes ultimate responsibility for waste storage. An AFR is to be constructed, although such important points as to when, where, and how still have to be worked out. Power companies may send their waste to the AFR—but only after a genuine and diligent effort to find their own means of storage and disposal. The Act says that the government must find and license a permanent resting place for nuclear waste by 1991. It may indeed be possible for the government to establish an AFR despite local protests. After all, there already are storage sites for nuclear waste, resulting from federal (mostly military) projects. But a key amendment allows states to veto storage sites within their borders. Both houses of Congress would have to overturn the veto. Observers wonder if even the power of a federal law will make a safe, permanent depository possible.

CONCLUSION

Once, nuclear power seemed to be a magic solution to society's ever increasing demand for energy. Now, nuclear energy seems less attractive. Some people wonder if it will be used at all within twenty years. The coming years will tell the story. Oil and coal continue to be used up. Will another oil shortage revive nuclear power's attractions? Will science discover a radioactive waste disposal method that is acceptable to all? Or will some terrible accident at a reactor convince people that nuclear power is an outlaw technology? We must wait for science and history to supply the answers.

CHRONOLOGY OF NUCLEAR ENERGY DEVELOPMENT

450 B.C.   The Greek philosopher Democritus advances the idea that tiny, indivisible particles of matter make up everything in the universe. He calls these particles *atoms,* a word meaning "cannot be cut."

1750   Benjamin Franklin identifies positive and negative charges of electricity.

1774   Antoine Lavoisier establishes the law of conservation of mass. This proved that matter cannot be destroyed. It led, in time, to Einstein's historic equation $E=mc^2$.

1803   John Dalton proposes the modern atomic theory. It is similar to Democritus's earlier guess. Dalton's work is based on actual observation.

1828   Jons Jacob Berzelius determines a table of atomic weights for all the then-known elements.

1895   Wilhelm Konrad Roentgen discovers X rays, setting the stage for the discovery of radioactivity.

1896   Becquerel discovers natural radioactivity.

1898	Marie and Pierre Curie discover polonium and radium, highly radioactive elements.
1905	Albert Einstein publishes his theory that matter and energy are equivalent.
1911	Ernest Rutherford discovers the nucleus of the atom.
1913	Frederick Soddy, working with Rutherford, discovers the existence of isotopes of elements.
1919	Rutherford succeeds in splitting an atom of nitrogen by bombarding it with alpha particles.
1931	Harold Urey discovers deuterium, a heavy isotope of hydrogen.
1932	James Chadwick discovers the neutron.
1934	Leo Szilard describes the possibility of a nuclear chain reaction in which each neutron bombarding a nucleus produces two or more neutrons, plus the release of energy.
1938	Otto Hahn and Fritz Strassmann bombard a uranium atom with neutrons and produce two separate elements, barium and krypton.
1939	Lisa Meitner and Otto Frisch publish a paper showing that Hahn and Strassmann had produced the first human-made nuclear fission reaction.
1942	Enrico Fermi directs the assembly and operation of the first atomic pile to produce a sustained nuclear chain reaction.
1945	The first atom bomb is exploded at Alamogordo, New Mexico. In the same year, similar bombs are dropped on Hiroshima and Nagasaki, in Japan, to end the war.
1946	The U.S. Atomic Energy Commission is established by law to control and promote nuclear energy development in the United States.

1949	The Soviet Union explodes its first atom bomb ending the U.S. monopoly on such weapons.
1952	The United States explodes the first hydrogen bomb, a fusion device, at a test site at Eniwetok, a small island in the Pacific Ocean.
1953	President Dwight D. Eisenhower announces the Atoms For Peace program. He also proposes that an international atomic energy agency be set up.
1954	The first nuclear submarine, christened *Nautilus*, is launched. Private industry in the United States is allowed to take over development of nuclear power.
1955	The First United Nations International Conference on Peaceful Uses of Atomic Energy meets in Geneva, Switzerland.
1957	The United Nations formally establishes the International Atomic Energy Agency. The Shippingport, Pennsylvania, Atomic Power Plant, first full-scale plant in the United States, develops rated power of 90 megawatts.
1959	The first nuclear merchant ship is launched at Camden, New Jersey. It is named the *Savannah,* in honor of the first steamship to cross the Atlantic. The first Polaris missile-launching submarine to be powered by nuclear energy is launched. It is christened the *George Washington.*
1961	The first nuclear power plant designed for use in outer space is sent into orbit.
1962	The first nuclear power plant to be used in the Antarctic is put into operation.
1963	President John F. Kennedy signs the Limited Test Ban Treaty for nuclear weapons.

1964   President Lyndon B. Johnson signs a law allowing the private ownership of nuclear materials for industrial and other uses.

1974   The functions of the Atomic Energy Commission are divided between the newly formed Energy Research and Development Administration and the Nuclear Regulatory Commission.

1977   The newly formed Department of Energy takes over all nuclear energy responsibilities for the United States.

1978   A Soviet nuclear-powered satellite falters and falls to earth in a sparsely populated area of northern Canada.

1979   An accident takes place at Three Mile Island, a nuclear power plant near Harrisburg, Pennsylvania.

1982   Congress passes the Nuclear Waste Policy Act of 1982. The law stipulates requirements for moving, storing, and disposing of nuclear wastes.

GLOSSARY

Atom. One of nature's "building blocks," a subunit of matter. An atom consists of a nucleus of neutrons and protons, surrounded by moving electrons.

Atomic Number. The number of protons or electrons in atoms of an element.

Atomic Pile. See **Nuclear Reactor.**

Atomic Weight. The total number of protons and neutrons in an atom's nucleus.

Away From Reactor Sites (AFRs). Temporary storage proposed for all the nuclear waste created until the end of the twentieth century. AFRs would be large storage pools, centrally located so as to hold the waste from many reactors.

Binding Energy. The energy holding the neutrons and protons in the atom's nucleus together.

Breeder Reactor. A reactor that produces more atomic fuel than it burns up.

Chain Reaction. The self-sustained fissioning of atoms in a material such as uranium 235 or plutonium 239.

Control Rods. Metal rods, such as those of cadmium, which control the fission process in a reactor by absorbing excess neutrons.

Coolant. A substance that conducts heat from a reactor core. Water, gas, nuclear fuel, and liquid metal are all used as coolants.

Core. The "furnace" of the nuclear reactor, where radioactive fuel is fissioned to produce heat.

Electron. A negatively charged atomic particle.

Element. Any one of the materials that make up our world that are not compounds, and whose atoms are all of the same type. Water is not an element because it is a combination of two types of atoms, hydrogen and oxygen.

Fallout, Radioactive. Particles carrying radioactive waste from nuclear explosions.

Fission. The splitting apart of an atomic nucleus, accompanied by the release of heat and radioactivity.

Gaseous Diffusion. A slow, expensive enrichment process that removes much of the uranium 238 from the processed ore, leaving the fissionable uranium 235. After enrichment, fuel contains about three times as much uranium 235 as uranium 238.

Half-Life. The time required for half of a given quantity of radioactive material to decay away.

Heavy Water. Water containing an isotope of hydrogen. Heavy water has a neutron in its hydrogen atom, which ordinary water (light water) does not have.

Isotope. A form of an element that contains an usual number of neutrons in the atomic nucleus. Heavy hydrogen is an isotope.

Meltdown. The hypothetical result of failure in a reactor's cooling system; the point at which the temperature in the reactor rises to 5,000°F (2,760°C), melting the uranium and releasing large amounts of radioactive materials into the atmosphere. Meltdown is also known as the "China syndrome."

Moderator. Material used to slow down the neutrons in a nuclear reactor. Graphite and heavy water are examples.

Molecule. A subunit of matter composed of atoms linked together. The atoms may be similar or different. If they are similar, they are molecules of an element. If they are different, they are molecules of a compound.

Neutron. A particle found in the atomic nucleus and also traveling between atoms. It weighs about the same as the proton but has no electrical charge.

Nuclear Energy. Energy released by nuclear reactions such as fission. It is far more powerful than chemical energy. Nuclear energy was once called atomic energy, but this term is not technically correct.

Nuclear Reactor. First called **Atomic Pile,** this is the container in which artificial fission can take place. It is the main device at a nuclear power plant. There are several types of reactors, but all use nuclear energy to turn water to steam, which is then used to produce electricity.

Nucleus. (pl. nuclei) The inner core of the atom, consisting of tightly packed protons and neutrons.

Plutonium. A radioactive metallic element. It is produced from uranium 238 and is used as a nuclear fuel.

Proton. A positively charged nuclear particle.

Radioactivity. The natural flow of nuclear radiation from a radioactive material.

Radium. A radioactive element far more powerful than uranium. It is found in the same ore but only in tiny amounts.

Reactor. See **Nuclear Reactor.**

Shielding. A layer of protective material around a reactor to prevent the release of radiation.

Thorium. A radioactive element used as a fertile material to produce nuclear fuel.

Uranium. A radioactive heavy element, two isotopes of which can be used as nuclear fuel.

FOR FURTHER READING

Adler, Irving. *Atomic Energy.* New York: John Day, 1971.

Ardley, Neil. *Atoms and Energy,* updated ed. New York: Franklin Watts, 1982.

Asimov, Isaac. *Inside the Atom*, rev. ed. New York: Abelard-Schuman, 1974.

_____. *How Did We Find Out About Nuclear Power?* New York: Walker, 1976.

Berger, Melvin. *Energy.* New York: Franklin Watts, 1983.

Goode, Stephen. *The Nuclear Energy Controversy.* New York: Franklin Watts, 1980.

Hawkes, Nigel. *Nuclear Energy.* New York: Franklin Watts, 1981.

Hyde, Margaret O. *Atoms Today and Tomorrow.* New York: McGraw-Hill, 1970.

Single copies of the following publications are available free from:

Technical Information Center
P.O. Box 62
Oak Ridge, Tennessee 37830

Angelo, Joseph A., Jr. *Stamps Tell the Nuclear Story.*

Asimov, Isaac. *Worlds Within Worlds: The Story of Nuclear Energy.* Vols. 1, 2, and 3.

Dukert, Joseph M. *Atoms on the Move: Transportation of Radioactive Materials.*

_____. *High Level Radioactive Waste: Safe Storage and Ultimate Disposal.*

INDEX